A Boy and a Turtle

A Children's Relaxation Story

Lori Lite

Illustrated by Kimberly C. Fox

I dedicate this book

to all the children

looking for the feeling of peace,

and to the parents who are willing

to help them find it.

I thank my children,

Tarin, Austin, and Jemma,

for infusing me with

the energy of unconditional love

and giving me the feeling of peace.

Collect the Indigo Dreams Series and watch your whole family manage anxiety, stress and anger...

CD/Audio Books:

Indigo Dreams

Indigo Ocean Dreams

Indigo Teen Dreams

Indigo Dreams: Garden of Wellness

Indigo Dreams: Adult Relaxation

Books:

A Boy and a Bear

The Goodnight Caterpillar

The Affirmation Web

A Boy and a Turtle

Children's Wellness Curriculum

Children's Stress Awareness Curriculum

Books, CDs, curriculums and other products designed to empower children, teens and adults are available at www.LiteBooks.net

Congratulations!

You have taken a wonderful step in bringing relaxation to your child.

A Boy and a Turtle is designed to relax your child's mind and body.
Both you and your child will learn a simple, fun visualization by working with colors. Your child will naturally follow the boy and turtle along as they fill their bodies with the colors of the rainbow.

Each time I read this story, I enjoy the feeling of peace. Even when hurried, the colors bathe me in a bath of serenity that is irresistible.

Visualizing is a lifelong technique that can be used for relaxation, healing, stress management, and overall well being. I invite you and your family to join me in the field of colors.

Lori Lite

A boy sat watching a quiet pond.

A rainbow danced at the water's edge.

A turtle on the other side of the pond

also noticed the rainbow.

The boy removed his shoes

and placed his feet into the warm water.

He shut his eyes and imagined

that the colors of the rainbow that filled the pond

could also fill his body.

The turtle, curious about what the boy was doing,

also put his feet into the warm water

and shut his eyes.

The boy drew a breath
of warm air in
through his nose
and felt all the stress
of the day slip away.

The turtle also drew

the warm air in

through his nose

and gave a gentle sigh

as he let the air out through his mouth.

The boy imagined that the color red
was flowing up from the pond into his feet,
making them float like petals on the water.

The turtle also felt the red flow into his feet
as he started to drift toward the boy.

The boy felt the red turn into orange as it traveled up his legs.

The orange allowed his legs to relax
and let go of all their tightness.

The turtle also felt the orange travel up his legs
as he drifted closer to the boy.

The boy felt the orange turn into yellow

as it warmed his stomach and chest.

The yellow filled his body with an inner glow.

The turtle also felt the yellow warm his body

as he drifted even closer to the boy.

The boy felt the yellow turn into green as it touched his heart and poured into his arms and hands.

The gentle green filled his heart with love and made his arms feel like blades of grass swaying in the breeze.

The turtle also felt the green touch his heart and pour into his arms and hands as he drifted still closer to the boy.

The boy felt the green turn into blue

as it explored his neck and jaw.

The blue felt peaceful, like the ocean rising with the tide.

The turtle also felt the blue explore his neck and jaw

as he drifted even closer to the boy.

The boy felt the blue turn into purple
as it swirled around his head.

The purple washed all the thoughts from his head,
leaving his mind completely still.

The turtle also felt the purple swirl around his head
as he drifted so close that his head touched the boy's hand.

The boy smiled, and together the boy and the turtle

felt the rainbow's colors embrace them

in a soothing white glow.

In their newfound oneness,

they knew that they had

experienced the wonder of colors.